If You Were Me and Lived in...
the Ancient Mali Empire

By Carole P. Roman

Illustrated by Mateya Arkova

For my grandmother who was our family's griot.

Special thanks to all the bloggers and homeschool moms who are spreading the word of this series.

I love grassroots movements!

Copyright 2015 Carole P. Roman All rights reserved.
ISBN-13:978-1540337276 ISBN-10:1540337278
Library of Congress Control Number: 2012921018
CreateSpace Independent Publishing Platform,
North Charleston, SC

If you were me and lived at the height of the Mali (Mah-lee) Empire, you would have been born in the year 1332. This was an important time in Mali. It was when it was considered a vital trade center and a world power.

From the year 1230 to around the early 1600s, the Mali Empire was also known as the Mandingo (Man-din-go) Empire.

The word Mali means hippopotamus (hip-uh-pot-uh-mus) in the Mandinka language.

This is a town in Mali today.

This is what a city in Mali may have looked like seven hundred years ago.

Mali started as a small part of the kingdom of Ghana (Ga-na) then rebelled against the government and became a kingdom in their own right.

The Kingdom of Mali emerged as the most powerful in the Western Sudan (Su-dan). The Mali Empire grew to extend over a large portion of Western Africa from the Atlantic Ocean to the southern part of the Sahara (Sah-ha-ruh) Desert.

With strong leadership, Mali was able to take control of trade routes, making the economy and people rich.

If you were a girl, your parents might have chosen the name Wassa (Wass-ah) or Mariam (Ma-ree-am). They might have given the names Dango (Dang-o) or Ibraham (Ib-rah-ham) to your brothers.

What do the names tell you about the Malian (Ma-lee-an) society?

You lived in the capital, Niani (Nee-an-ee). It had a major road that ran through it that was as long as it was wide. It was an important road because it was the road to Mecca (Mek-ca) as well. Mecca was a special city important to the followers of Islam (Is-lam).

Many people in your country embraced the Islam faith. Some still followed the old way, but your grandfather became a Muslim (Mus-lim) when the king changed his religion. You knew that your family was part of the Mande (Man-dee) people and spoke a language called Mandinka (Man-din-ka).

You lived in a large home made with mud bricks and an adobe (ah-do-bee) plaster. It had large wooden log support beams that jutted out of the walls on the outside of the house. It had multiple rooms with carved out passageways between them. The earthen walls made the house cool in the hot summer months.

The houses were round-shaped with grass domed roofs. Some of the newer homes had completely flat rooftops, making the houses look like squat, square boxes.

You shared the house with your father and his four wives. There were seventeen children between all your father's wives. He always told you that you were his favorite daughter!

You had heard that recently the government had ordered that many of the palaces were to be converted into mosques (mosks).

Mosques were places for people who follow Islam to pray.

They built mosques from rice husks, earth, and water. The mud was sun dried. They were four stories high and had three minarets (min-a-rets), which are tall towers where people are called to daily prayer.

People loved to go to pray in the beautiful mosques. You knew that if people didn't get to the mosque early on Friday, it would be crowded and hard to find a spot in the large building.

These sixty-foot high towers were topped with ostrich eggs, which were put there for good fortune and fertility.

Mali was a lovely place to live. You enjoyed the dry, desert-like weather.

The Niger (Nie-jher) River was nearby and served as a vital source for fresh fish, water, and trade between towns.

Your older brother told you about other important places in the Mali Empire that made it special.

He went to the great city of Timbuktu (Tim-buck-too) to go to school. Timbuktu was world-famous. It had a huge university with a enormous library containing ancient Greek and Roman books. People traveled there from all over the world.

Kangaba (Kan-ga-ba) was the spiritual capital, which meant that it was an important religious center where people came to feel a kinship with each other.

Your brother described the major trade routes that cut through central Mali bearing salt from the Sahara Desert in the north and gold in the south. These groups were made up of caravans. There were hundreds of camels loaded for products that people traded for the best resources in Mali: salt from the desert and gold from the mines.

Traders brought silk, captured slaves, and many other products from China and Europe. Mali needed the slaves to work in the salt and gold mines. Europe and Asia needed salt to preserve their meat so that it would taste good and last long. They needed Mali's gold to create coins for their currency.

You weren't sure which was more valuable, the salt or gold. Either way, you knew your father had a lot of both, which made you wealthy.

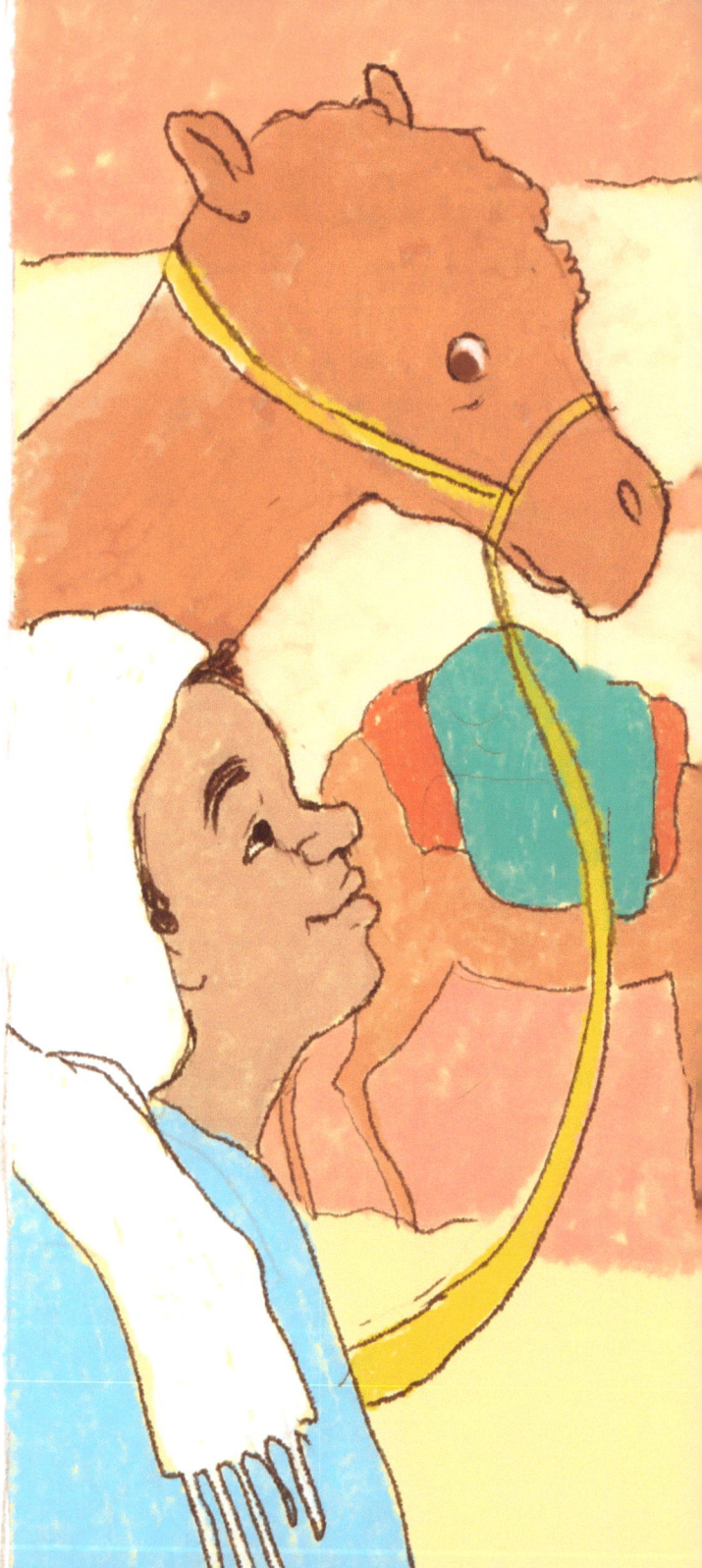

Both your grandfather and father were important people in the government. Because of this you lived near the royal palace.

The palace was a large compound that served as the king's home and where all the government offices were. There were meeting rooms, guest rooms, servants quarters, a stable, and a cooking area that was able to make feasts for thousands of people.

In this palace lived Mansa Musa (Man-sa Moo-sa). Mansa was another name for the king or emperor. Musa was his given name. The name Musa is Moses in Islam. Have you heard of that name?

Your brother had secretly taken you to see the king's throne on a special day when the leader was holding court. You hid behind a pillar because girls were not supposed to be there.

You gasped when you saw the mighty king. He looked magnificent in a red velvet tunic and a golden skullcap. He sat on the polished black throne. It was high on a rectangular platform at one end of the courtyard. It was carved from ebony and had two huge ivory tusks on either side, standing like guards.

A servant held a large silk umbrella over the king's head, shading him from the sun. There were two servants behind him, fanning him constantly.

There were musicians with drums made from stretched goatskin and gourds in all different sizes. Some men strummed on a kora (kor-a), which was an instrument that had a long neck and twenty-one strings. There were several flutes made from millet stalks, bamboo, and gourds.

You loved to close your eyes and move to the pleasant rhythms.

The king gave orders, and his dyeli (die-ale-ee) or herald would shout them out to the crowd. He served as the king's voice as well as a master of ceremonies for court functions and festivals.

Behind them, there were horses lined up in case the king wanted to leave.

You spotted your father. He stood near the king as a military advisor should. He had to give reports often to the leader.

The area was filled with hundreds of people waiting to hear what Mansa Musa had to say.

In this courtyard, you watched the great king listen to disputes and give out orders.

The king spent the day listening to people argue over disagreements. Sometimes it was about cattle, other times a fight over land. Either way, the sun was hot, and the discussions were long and boring.

After all the disputes had been settled, your grandfather was called to the center of the courtyard.

Your grandfather was known for his long memory. Since there was no written language, history was told by a storyteller called a griot (gree-oh) whose job was to memorize it. Your grandfather became the most famous griot in the land. He was ordered to come and live near the palace to be available to the king.

The king nodded, and your grandfather cleared his throat to start the story. He took a deep breath then began the great tale of Mandinka people.

Your grandfather sang in a booming voice that he received his knowledge from his father, who learned it from his own father going back in time to when the people made their lives on the banks of the Niger River.

The ancient people had divided into twelve clans with twelve kings to govern each group. Castes were created consisting of hunters, blacksmiths, and artisans. The castes were established, he explained, so that everyone would know their place in society.

Fighting broke out, and there was chaos. For a long time there was war, which created poverty and hunger. The twelve kings formed a royal council and picked a mansa to rule over them all.

The mansa was to be all-powerful and rule all of the Mandinka tribes. This brought peace.

For many years the Mandinka people prospered. Then the droughts came. There was no rain, and all the crops died. Life was hard. Your grandfather continued the history of your people. He was crying when he told this part of the story.

Animals were dying; the river dried up. People were starving. The king at the time, Mansa Barmandana (Ba-ra-man-da-na), was told that if he embraced Islam, the drought would end.

He converted, and the rain came. The lands turned lush and green. There was great prosperity, which meant people grew wealthy and had plenty to eat.

Many people followed his lead and converted to the new religion as well.

It was so quiet you could hear your heart beating. No one made a sound.

Your grandfather stopped talking. He raised his hands to the sky. He said in a soft voice, "One day terrible storm darkened the sky. The storm foretold the birth of a great leader. Then the lion child was born," he roared this part into the silent courtyard. All eyes were on your grandfather.

"The Almighty made the thunder peal, the sky light up, and the earth shake." He walked the length of the long courtyard.

You noticed that nobody was moving. Every person was listening intently to your grandfather.

Even Mansa Musa sat forward, his chin on his hand, his eyes sharp.

"Sundiata Keita (Sun-die-at-a Ket-a) was the bravest prince to ever have lived." Your grandfather called out. "He was Mansa Musa's grandfather, and his name meant Hungering Lion."

Your grandfather told of Sundiata's inability to walk when he was a child. You marveled at the story of how a blacksmith made braces for his legs, and the young prince taught himself to walk upright. Through hard work and exercise, he became the finest archer in the land. He studied history and law.

After a while, he was chosen to lead the army to overthrow an evil king. He united the many tribes, and together they began the Mali Empire. He took control of the valuable salt and gold mines, making the people thrive and grow rich.

Everyone stood and cheered. This was the birth of your nation, and it filled you with pride. You smiled to yourself because you had heard it a hundred times directly from your grandfather himself.

You liked to listen when he taught your little brother to be the next griot in the family.

As your grandfather prepared your brother, so his legacy continued; so did Sundiata Keita pave the way for his descendant, Mansa Musa.

Sundiata united the people, leaving a flourishing land for the next king.

Mansa Musa continued his grandfather's plans by defeating the bandits who roamed the countryside ruining trade. This increased business, making Mali very rich.

He was a just and fair ruler, encouraging all religions to be practiced. While he converted and followed Islam, he allowed religious tolerance in the kingdom, enabling people to worship as they pleased.

Many people continued with both religions, combining Muslim beliefs with local traditions.

Mansa Musa created the most informational seat of learning in Timbuktu, inviting scholars from all over the world to exchange knowledge, making his country important to world development. He made education free for students.

As you watched your grandfather speak, your mouth opened in wonder, as everybody bowed deeply to their great leader.

Your father was an important general in the army. He served Mansa Musa directly and led the army that guarded the gold mines. They were responsible for watching the trade routes. He had as much as 90,000 men on duty at any one time. You knew the army had a wide variety of weapons to defend their riches.

They used bows and barbed, poisoned-tipped arrows. Each warrior had a shield made from animal hide. Most carried a stabbing spear called a tamba (tam-ba). The soldiers were a fearsome sight, and you knew they kept your home as well as the roads safe.

Your father looked grand in his chainmail armor. You watched as the courtyard was cleared and the best warriors came forward to show their fighting skills in front of the mansa.

While your father was the head of your clan, he had many brothers that held other professions.

Many of your relatives worked on the river, unloading cargo, or as sailors bringing products to your city. They had large herds of cattle that served as a food source in the markets.

The most respected job was that of a farmer. The farmers lived on the fertile land of the Niger River, tending the land to provide food for everyone. Some of your cousins lived away from the city in the countryside. They grew peanuts, cotton, and grains. In the winter, they served in the army, and in the summer, they returned to farming.

Below the farmers were the artisans. They were craftsmen that created pottery and sculptures for worship. Some made things with leather. Other groups included soldiers, fisherman, and civil servants who worked for the government. Lastly were the unfortunate slaves who were captured to work in the gold and salt mines.

Slaves were brought in from the Sahara by the caravans traveling from different parts of the world. You knew that Mali was an important part of the Arab slave trade. There were raids where people from nearby lands were captured and made into slaves. It was sad, but slaves were considered a valuable commodity rather than people.

You heard your father complain that Mali was growing so big that Mansa Musa couldn't hear all of the complaints of the people.

Your father suggested dividing the areas into provinces. Mansa Musa agreed. He put governors called ferbas (fur-bus) in charge of each area. Each village had a mayor. Day to day problems would be taken care of locally, and Mansa Musa could govern the growing Empire.

There were inspectors called mochrifs (moch-rifs) and royal tax collectors. Mali was organized and ran well. People had money and plenty to eat.

Your father had to travel from town to town to make sure problems were handled fairly and the citizens were doing their job.

You knew that the citizens were afraid to break the law. The punishment was fierce and fast. Liars had their tongues cut out; thieves lost their hands. People learned it was better to follow the rules, so the land was peaceful.

People loved to come and visit Mali. The roads were safe, and visitors were always welcome.

Your father traveled a lot, and you didn't see him often. You were used to this. Children were usually the responsibility of their mother until they turned twelve.

Boys went to school in mosques where they were taught to recite the Quran (Kor-an). They could also learn a craft or trade by the time they were twelve.

Girls stayed home with their mothers where they learned how to be good wives and mothers.

You were fed, cosseted, and kept safe. You felt pampered and loved by your parents.

However, you knew the time was coming soon for you to marry.

When your second oldest brother turned twelve, he had a ceremony to make him a man. You were glad when this finally happened; he was prone to acting like a baby and pulling your hair.

He moved to the next town and was apprenticed to your uncle, who was artisan. Your brother had to learn a profession to earn money. Your uncle made ceremonial statues for people to worship.

He carved statues from wood with exaggerated features famous in Mali art. He was an excellent artist, and you marveled at his talent. Your brother was lucky he had a good teacher. He came home with many finely carved statues. You were surprised at how talented he was. All you thought he was capable of doing was annoying you.

Twelve to thirteen was a turning point for you too. You would be considered ready to have children, and a marriage would be arranged.

A young man would take three kola (ko-la) nuts to your father when he decided to ask to marry you. They would argue about the amount of nuts for your hand in marriage, eventually settling on ten kola nuts. He would bring an entire basket of them on your wedding day.

A kola nut is a bitter fruit with pale flesh inside. Everybody loves the feeling they get when they eat the nuts. It makes them wide awake and full of energy.

Family members would send gifts of cloth to your mother for you to build your wardrobe. Men would give money to the bridegroom your parents had chosen for you.

You knew your bridegroom's family would have to pay for the wedding.

You had time to worry about the thought of a husband. You were just ten this last year.

You liked to dress up with all the beautiful printed clothes your mother had in her room.

Mali was known for its unique tie-dye and mud cloths. Traditional designs were painted or pounded by stamps on sheets of rough cloth, using different types of soil for color. Only females worked on the cloth to make these designs.

All the women wore a wraparound skirt called a pagne (pan-yuh) with a matching tunic and headdress.

Your mother came from a town where the women wore eight small rings on the rim of her ear to signify her eight ancestors. She wore grisgris (gri-gri) to make evil spirits go away. A grisgris was a lucky charm to ward off evil spirits. You wore a charm under your tunic (too-nik) that your grandmother made for you. The grisgris was on a leather string and tied around your neck.

All of your father's wives wore an assortment of amulets, bracelets, and rings. After all, how else could you show how wealthy you were? You loved mixing the traditions of your African ancestors with your new Muslim faith.

You enjoyed the vibrant and loud colors of the clothes. Women could choose whether or not they wanted to cover their hair in the Muslim tradition. The king declared people could live they way the wanted and worship as they choose.

Men mostly wore the boubou (boo-boo), a full length tunic.

Mansa Musa favored baggy pants. In fact, it was a high honor if a man wore baggy pants, the bigger, the greater the honor. Your father had a pair of pants so big, he could hide all his children behind them. This proved he was a great man.

One of your uncles wore a hunter's tunic. It was a tunic decorated with animal claws, shells, teeth, and fur. It had many secret pockets with amulets to ward off evil spirits as well as dangerous animals.

He wore it to the many festivals and celebrations to remind people of how powerful your family was.

There was one tradition that you weren't allowed to participate in. When someone in the family died, only men could accompany the body to the cemetery if the person was a Muslim. This made you angry when your great-grandmother passed away.

You had to stay home when they buried her.

You were never hungry.

Rice and a thick porridge made of millet were at every meal.

Breakfast was a combination of grounded millet, tamarind (tam-er-ind), and sugar mixed with milk to make a porridge. It is called bouille (bowl-le). It was like a runny rice pudding.

Your cook made a sauce of fresh vegetables, fish, meat, or chicken to eat with the porridge.

Small pancakes made from millet were prepared too. Millet was a grain that was affordable to all people. You knew your were wealthy because rice was always available. Poor people ate only the millet.

Dinner was grilled fish caught fresh from the Niger River. The captaine fish was your favorite. You also loved to eat tinani (tin-an-ee), another small fish. You also ate goat, lamb, chicken, and whatever meat was found in the large market in town. Your cook went daily to buy the food fresh. Refreshing juices from the hibiscus (hi-bis-kis) flower, ginger, or the fruit of the baobab (bay-o-bab) tree were always on the table.

You loved when the great king went out for rides to visit his kingdom. He traveled with many of your father's guards as well as an entire troupe of acrobats for entertainment.

The king was a generous and beloved man. He gave out gifts wherever he went, offering beautiful cloth to nuggets of gold. He believed wealth should be shared.

He was the most famous mansa in your history. Mansa Musa gained this fame because he worked to promote his country to the world. His mission was to make the world aware of the greatness of Mali.

He traveled to Mecca in Saudi Arabia on a lavish trip, bringing a huge entourage of over 60,000 people. He went there on a hajj (haj) or pilgrimage in the year 1324. Muslims worldwide make this special trip to pray at one of the most holiest sites in their faith.

The mansa went with tons of gold, spending so much that it brought a lot of attention to his country. He returned with scholars, artists, architects, and teachers and as many new ideas to improve life in Mali.

Mansa Musa doubled the size of Mali.

It was said that Mansa Musa was the wealthiest man in the world at that time.

Although Mali was known for its gold, it did not produce any minted coins. You knew salt was traded for goods in the marketplace.

Only the king could use gold nuggets for trade; everybody else had to use gold dust. Many used salt for trading; it was as good as gold.

Salt was broken off large bricks and sought after people in the southern part of the country. Mali is a hot climate, and salt is needed to replenish the minerals in humans when they sweat from the heat.

Women were allowed to operate stalls in the vast and noisy marketplace. There were no set prices, so people had to be good at haggling.

There was always a good supply of kola nuts in the house for important people. You gave them to guests as a sign of respect. Sometimes you brought them as gifts.

You knew many of the nuts came to your father as gifts from people who appreciated his fairness with them when he was out on the king's business.

Famous people in the Mali Empire:

Inari Kunate (In-ar-ie Kun-ate)- Mansa Musa's senior wife. She is famous because she went with him on his pilgrimage to Mecca.

Kongo (Kon-go)- Mansa Musa's mother. Mandinka people were a matriarchal society, which meant that a person's family history was traced through his mother's side.

Abu Ishaq Ibrahim Al-Sahili (Ah-bu Is-shak Ib-rah-ham Al-Sah-il-ee)(1290–1346)-A prominent architect of the Mali Empire under the rule of Mansa Musa. He helped build the Great Mosque of Gao and the Royal Palace in Timbuktu.

Maghan Kon Fatta (Ma-gan Kon Fat-tah) (d. 1218)- A Mandinka king. He was the father of Sundiata, who brought Islam to the Mali Kingdom.

Sassouma Bereté (Sass-ou-ma Ber-et)- First wife of famous Mansa Maghan Kon Fatta. She hated his son Sundiata- she embarrassed and insulted Sundiatta.

Sologon (So-lo-gon)- The favorite wife of Maghan Kon Fatta and Sundiata's mother. When Maghan Kon Fatta died, she was forced to live in a storage hut, eventually fleeing.

Muhammad Ibn Battuta (Mo-ham-id Ib-in Bat-tu-uah) February 25, 1304 – 1368 or 1369)- is known for his travels throughout the Middle East. He was a scholar who recorded his travels in a book. Ibn Battuta visited most of the Islamic world as well as many of the non-Muslim countries over a 30-year time period. His journeys included trips to West Africa, North Africa, Middle East, the Horn of Africa, South Asia, Central Asia, Southeast Asia and China.

Farim-Soura (Far-eem Soor-rah)- A commander in the Mali army. He was an advisor to the king. The army was divided into two parts of north and south. It was said that between the two generals they commanded 100,000 men.

Sankar-Zouma (San-kar Zoo-mah) - Another commander in the Mali army. He was also an advisor to the king who worked with Soura.

Shihāb al-Dīn Abū al-'Abbās Aḥmad B. Faḍl Allāh al-'Umarī (Shee-hab al Din A-bu Ab-bas-Ah-mad) (1300 – 1349)- An Arab historian who was born in Damascus. Al-Umari visited Cairo after the Mansa Musa's pilgrimage to Mecca. His writings are one of the best sources for this hajj. Al-Umari recorded that the Mansa gave away so much gold that its value fell in Egypt for years afterward.

Glossary

acrobats (ack-roe-bats)- people who are talented at tumbling, walking on stilts, or tight-rope walking.

adobe (a-do-bee)- a brick or building material of sun-dried earth and straw.

advisor (ad-vise-or)- one who consults and gives advice.

amulet (am-u-lit)- a small item that is worn to protect a person from things such as illness and misfortune.

ancestors- (an-ces-tors)- the people from whom a person is descended.

archer (arch-er)- a person who knows how to use a bow and arrow.

architects (ar-ki-tects)- those who design buildings.

artisan (art-a-son)- a craftsperson experienced in a trade or field, notably using their hands.

bandits (band-its)- thieves.

baobab (bay-o-bab) - a tree that grows a tasty fruit. It has a fat little trunk and can live thousands of years.

Barmandana (Bar-man-dan-a)- the first Muslim king of the Mali Empire in 1397 AD.

boubou (boo-boo)- a full-length tunic, usually colorful.

bouille (bowl-le)- a runny rice pudding.

braces (bra-ses)- two metal rods tied onto crooked legs to make them grow straight.

captaine (cap-i-tain)- a fish from Africa.

caravans (ker-uh-vans)- a group of pack animals used as transportation to sell and trade goods from town to town.

castes (casts)- people divided into classes, defining their place in society.

ceremonial (ser-e-mo-ni-al)- a formal event that could be political or religious.

chaos (ka-os)- an unorganized mess.

clans (klans)- a group of people, usually families, who are identified as part of a common group.

commodity (co-mod-i-tee)- something of worth that can be traded.

convert (cun-vert)- to change from one religion to another.

cosset (cos-it)- to pamper, spoil, and treat tenderly with care.

craftsmen (krafts-men)- an exceptionally skilled person who has much practice in their craft.

Dango (Dang-o)- a popular boy's name in Ancient Mali.

descendant (de-sen-dent)- a person who is descended from a particular ancestor.

droughts (drouts)- a lengthy amount of time that passes without rainfall, creating a shortage of water supply.

dyeli (die-ale-ee)- a loyal advisor who makes announcements for the king.

ebony (eb-on-nee)- black or dark brown wood that comes from a tropical tree.

emperor (em-per-er)- a man who rules an empire.

entourage (un-tur-raje)- a group of people who travel and aid an important person.

exaggerated (ig-za-jer-ated)- inflated far beyond the truth.

ferbas (fur-bus)- a regional official who takes care of a group of villages.

fertile (fur-til)- farmable land that yields a lot of crops.

fertility (fur-til-ity)- the ability to reproduce.

festivals (fes-ti-vals)- celebrations that can be religious or to honor an event.

flourishing (flur-ish-ing)- having rapid growth and success.

foretold (for-told)- telling the future.

Ghana (Ga-na)- an ancient kingdom in ancient Africa.

ginger (jin-jer)- a hot fragrant spice made from a plant.

gourds (gords)- large fruit with hard skin.

governor (gov-er-nor)- a leader of a city or region.

griot (gree-oh)- a person who maintains a history of his family or tribe through memorization and recites it orally.

grisgris (gri-gri)- a lucky charm that protects the wearer from evil.

haggling (hag-el-ing)- negotiating over the cost of an item.

hajj (haj)- the Muslim pilgrimage to Mecca that takes place in the last month of the year; all Muslims are expected to make at least once during their lifetime.

headdress (hed-dress)- an ornamental head covering worn during ceremonies or for fashion.

herald (her-ald)- an official who tells the news of the king.

hibiscus (hi-bis-kis)- a plant with big, bright, beautiful flowers.

hippopotamus (hip-uh-pot-uh-mus)- a large, thick-skinned semi-aquatic African mammal with massive jaws and large tusks.

Ibraham (Ib-rah-ham)- a popular boy's name in ancient Mali.

Islam (Is-lam)- the religion of the Muslims, a monotheistic faith regarded as revealed through Muhammad as the prophet of Allah.

Kangaba (Kan-ga-ba)- an important city in Ancient Mail. It was known as the spiritual center of the kingdom.

kinship (kin-ship)- relationship or a feeling of closeness.

kola (ko-la)- a nut from a small evergreen tree in Africa.

kora (kor-a)- a large instrument with a long neck and twenty-one strings which played similar to a harp by plucking the strings.

lavish (lav-ish)- costly and expensive.

legacy (leg-uh-see)- an inheritance or birthright.

Mali (Mah-lee) Empire- a successful West African empire that controlled trade routes throughout the thirteenth and fourteenth centuries.

Malian (Ma-lee-an)- the people who live in Mali.

Mande (Man-dee)- the people who speak a group of African languages; largely spoken in Mali, Guinea, and Sierra Leone.

Mandingo (Man-din-go)- a group of people belonging to West Africa.

Mandinka (Man-din-ka)- the people who speak a group of African languages; largely spoken in Senegal, Gambia, and Sierra Leone.

Mansa Musa (Man-sa Moo-sa)- an emperor who ruled the Mali Empire throughout the

14th century.

Mariam (Ma-ree-am)- a popular girl's name in ancient Mali.

master of ceremonies (master of cer-e-mon-ees)- a person who introduces speakers, players, or entertainers.

mayor (may-or)- an elected head of a town or city.

Mecca (Mek-ca)- a city in western Saudi Arabia, considered by Muslims to be the holiest city of Islam.

millet (mill-et)- the small-seeded grass used as grains for people to make food or beer.

minaret (min-a-ret)- the tall narrow towers apart of a mosque with a balcony where people are called to pray.

minerals (min-eh-rals)- the natural substances formed underground.

minted (mint-ed)- making currency with government authorization.

mochrifs (moch-rifs)- tax collectors and inspectors of an influential town within the kingdom of Mali.

mosques (mosk)- a place of Muslim worship.

Muslim (Mus-lim)- a follower of the religion of Islam.

Niani (Nee-an-ee)- the capital of Mali.

Sahara (Sah-ha-uh)- what is known as the largest desert in the world, located in North Africa and covers the continent from the Atlantic coast to the Red Sea.

Saudi Arabia (Sau-dee A-ra-bee-ya)- an Arab country in the Middle East, covering most of the Arabian Peninsula and ruled by a king.

scholar (skal-er)- a person who has studied a subject for a long time and knows a lot about it; an intelligent and well-educated person who knows a particular subject well.

skullcap (skull-cap)- a small close-fitting cap without a brim.

squat (skwat)- short and thick.

Sudan (Su-dan)- a country in North Africa, north of the equator and south of Egypt.

tamarind (tam-er-ind)- the sticky brown pulp from a pod from a tree that is used for flavoring food.

tamba (tam-ba)- a stabbing spear.

Timbuktu (Tim-buck-too)- a town close to the Niger River in Mali.

tinani (tin-an-ee)- a small fish from Africa.

tolerance (tol-er-ance)- allowing different beliefs to exist together.

traditions (trad-di-shuns)- the passing on or teaching customs or beliefs from generation to generation.

tunic (too-nik)- a loose garment, typically sleeveless and reaching to the wearer's knees.

tusks (tusks)- long, pointed teeth, as those on the elephant.

university (u-ni-ver-si-tee)- a school for higher education.

Wassa (Wass-ah)- a popular girl's name in Mali.